WOMEN WHO YOU ARE IN CHRIST!

BY

Joletha Cobb
N.C.C.A. Licensed Pastoral Clinical Counselor

Women
Who You Are In Christ
ISBN 978-0-6151-3540-3

Published By Joletha Cobb Ministries

Copyright © 2006 By Joletha Cobb Ministries

All rights reserved. No part of this book may be reproduced or transmitted in any form without the prior permission of the publisher/author.

Unless otherwise noted, Scripture quotations in this volume are from the New King James Version, Copyright © 1982 by Thomas Nelson, Inc. Used by permission.
All rights reserved.

Printed in the United States of America

TABLE OF CONTENTS

Dedication... 4
Forward 5

Chapter 1   Is God Prejudice?................................6
Chapter 2   Biblical Women of the Bible............15
Chapter 3   Women in The 21ˢᵗ Century............28
Chapter 4   Knowing God 40
Chapter 5   Women: Who Are We in Marriage 50
Chapter 6   Women In Abusive Marriages 61
Chapter 7   Women: Who We Are As Mothers 72
Chapter 8   Salvation 82

DEDICATION

I would like to dedicate this book first to God for giving me the inspiration and the words to say. He has always been a big part of my life and He has never deserted me when I needed Him. Thank you O Lord for helping me to survive the hard times and for saving me!

To my husband, Hank, I would like to say thank you for always supporting me in everything I do. I feel very blessed by God for a husband like you. I love you very much.

I also would like to dedicate this book to my mom, Bea Sigle. You have been an inspiration for some of this book. You have overcome a lot in your lifetime and remained strong. Thank you Mom for keeping my siblings and me in church all of our lives, for without the Word of God being a big part of our lives we would not be who we are today. Without your guidance we may not have made it through. Thank you Mom and I love you!

A word to my sister, Charlotte Cobb, would be that you were my strength throughout the hard times in our lives. Thank you for protecting us. It took a big part of your life away from you to do this. You were there for me then and I would like to be there for you now, for you are my best friend! I love you!

To my children, Terry, Teramie, and Canaan, I would like to say how proud I am of you all for giving your lives to Christ. It is a mother's dream to see all of her children saved. I am truly blessed to have such awesome children. I love you all very much!

Thanks to my brother Shawn Carroll for all of the support you have given me with this book and for your help designing the back cover for this book. I love you very much!

FORWARD

I am a licensed pastoral clinical counselor and I felt God leading me to write this Bible study on the identity of women in God's eyes. Women have been confused for many years just where they fit in, in this life. This book touches on subjects of who women are in themselves, who they are in God, and who they are in marriage. This book provides a chapter on the issue of domestic violence that is so prevalent in these last days. I felt God's leading on the writing of this book and this is based on what I believe is my true and accurate understanding of Scripture of God's Word. I do urge the readers of this book to pray for God's guidance for understanding of these Scriptures. I would never want to intentionally mislead anyone. So please, study the Scriptures that are listed in the book and allow yourselves to be led by the Holy Spirit for understanding.

I pray this book will give you some understanding and insight on how important you are in God's eyes. This I hope will help you to celebrate who you are and why you were created. I hope this book helps you to develop a closer relationship with Christ and renew your Spirit.

Most importantly, I hope this book will provide those who are in marriages consisting of abuse and violence to have the courage to seek help. I urge you to read Chapter 6 and to pray about your situation and let God intervene in your life. If I can help one woman who is in these violent relationships to be able to get help then this book will be serving the purpose that God had intended it for.

I pray you will receive a great blessing from this book! I want you to celebrate being the women of God you are! I know you will be truly blessed in the Lord by seeking a closer relationship with Him as He desires us to do.

"Draw nigh to God, and He will draw nigh to you." James 4:8

WOMEN WHO YOU ARE IN CHRIST!

Chapter 1

Is God Prejudice?

This book is being written to all those women who are wondering just exactly who they are in Christ. Is God prejudice? It is my desire to help women to know who they are in Christ and how important their role is in our society, in Christ's body and in the church, not only as daughters, wives, and mothers, but also as teachers, and children of God.

As daughters, some of us have been taught that our role as women is to marry and have children. As mothers, some of us have been taught that we should stay at home and raise our children without the possibility of a career. As wives, some of us have been taught that it is our job to raise children and keep house and do laundry and everything else that goes with being housewives. Some housewives have married very controlling men and have been in, and continue to be, in relationships with a lot of domestic violence involved. This has caused great harm to women as far as their safety and self-esteem.

I am not talking about those with marriages that are functioning properly but those marriages where there is great dysfunction and turmoil. These are the women who I want to address. Those women who have fear of getting up in the mornings, wondering what the day will be like; those women who have to ask permission from her mate to see her family or to go to the grocery store; those women who don't even have access to use the telephone without permission or have friends.

I will be discussing the subject of domestic violence and marriage in a Chapter 6. As a pastoral clinical counselor I want to show these and all women what their role is in Christ.

I wanted to write this study for those women who are in a relationship that is full of domestic violence and control. I am writing this book for those women who have such low self-esteem that it keeps them in spiritual bondage. I am writing this book for those women who are in great relationships or marriages at this time but still have a need to know who they are and how much they are worth in God's eyes. I am writing this book for those women who have a deep desire to live according to God's Word and be all they can be. **I am writing this book for *all* women**. It is God's desire to bless women with the knowledge of how they can be a vessel for His Glory. He wants to teach us how to be good daughters, wives, mothers, and best of all great children of God.

This study is written by my understanding of the Scripture and you should always make sure you study the Scriptures on your own and yield to the Holy Spirit for guidance and understanding. I don't ever want to mislead you because of my interpretation so I do urge you to complete the study guide after each chapter and read the Scriptures for your own understanding under God's guidance.

With that being said, let's look at the first Scripture in this study, which is:

Galatians 5:1. NKJV *"Stand fast therefore in the liberty by which Christ has made us free, and do not be entangled again with a yoke of bondage."*

This Scripture is telling us that we don't have to be slaves of bondage. We are free in Christ. NU-TEXT reads, "For freedom Christ has made us free; stand fast therefore."

Some women today are held in bondage. Whether it is the bondage of low self-esteem, depression, spiritual bondage, or bondage of a marriage that isn't working out, but due to religious beliefs is unable to get out of the marriage. God does not want us to live in bondage of any sort. He made us free. Free to serve Him, free to love Him, and free to love ourselves.

There are more women today than any other time that are living with low self-esteem. They are suffering from depression and despair. They are not sure who they are and what their role is in life and in God's eyes. God treasures you. You are His child. He wants you to believe in yourselves and know that you are truly important in His eyes.

Is God prejudice against women? This answer is an emphatic NO! This next verse will prove this.

Galatians 3:28 *says "There is neither Jew nor Greek, there is neither slave nor free, there is neither male nor female; for you are all one in Christ Jesus.*

This verse describes how Christ breaks down the barriers. This provides us with unity in Christ. This shows how there is no prejudice against race, gender, or social background. We are all one in Christ Jesus. This is a very freeing verse. This verse shows how God looks at us all the same. He holds no prejudice against women.

We can see through these Scriptures that God has made us all equally.

Genesis 1:27 says, *"So God created man in His own image; in the image of God He created him; male and female He created them."* He later tells ***them*** in ***Genesis 1:28*** *and says, " then God blessed **them**, and God said to **them**, "Be fruitful and multiply; fill the earth and subdue it; have dominion over every living thing."*

God also makes another statement that pertains to man and women being as one.
*Genesis 2:24 says, "Therefore a man shall leave his father and mother and shall be joined with his wife, and; **they shall become one flesh.***

In this first chapter we can see that God did not put women on earth to be held in bondage of any kind. He put Eve here as a companion for Adam.

Genesis *2:18 says, "And the Lord said, it is not good that a man should be alone; I will make him a helper."*

This statement was not meant to be prejudice or condescending. God wanted us to have relationships with others. He wants us to have a relationship with Him, as does He wants to have a relationship with us. We are here to have a relationship with God. He wants to have as good a personal relationship with women as He does with men.

A relationship is not full of prejudice. It is accepting one another as they are and appreciating the differences we all have.

Before we can accept ourselves we are to love ourselves.

We have to love ourselves before we can love anyone else. God wants us to love ourselves as women or men, no matter what our gender is.

Jeremiah 1:5 states, *"Before I formed you in the womb, I knew you; before you were born I sanctified you; I ordained you a prophet to the nations.*

Pray about this chapter and let God lead you to understanding. Yield to the Holy Spirit and follow His leading. As I stated earlier, this book is written by what I believe to be my true understanding of the Word of God.

There are also a few pages after each study exercise for you to journal your thoughts down. Write down what you have received out of each chapter you read. After all, this book is to help you learn to be what God wants you to be.

I John 4:15-16 says, "Whoever confesses that Jesus is the Son of God, God abides in Him, and he in God. And we have known and believed the love that God has for us. God is love, and he who abides in love abides in God and, God in him.

Here God is saying WHOEVER confesses that Jesus is the Son of God; WHOEVER meaning anyone; man or woman.

We have to appreciate the fact of being women and be joyous in that fact. We have to celebrate the truth of our womanhood. We have to be proud of who we are. We are children of God no matter what our gender is. He loves us all equally!

Go on to the Bible study exercise. Read the Scriptures and answer each question.

This prayer has been provided for you to help you to ask for God's understanding while studying this chapter. There is a prayer at the end of each chapter.

Dearest Heavenly Father,

It is my great desire to understand my position in your eyes. Please help me to yield my spirit to Your Holy Spirit for complete understanding. Open my eyes to help me to see the value of my life to you. I know you want me to carry out your will in this life you have given me. I want to fulfill all that you have for me to do. Please make known to me the plan you have for my life. As I meditate on these Scriptures, I am beginning to see that you are an impartial God who loves me no matter what my gender is and that I am more than a woman in your eyes, I am a child of God. Thank you for giving me the opportunity to be a part of your ministry and your divine plan.

In Jesus' Precious, Holy Name,
Amen.

Memory Scripture: **Galatians 3:8**, *"For you are all one in Christ Jesus."*

Chapter 1

Is God Prejudice?

Study Exercise 1

1. Read Galatians 5:1 and describe in your own words what your view on this verse is?
   _____
   _____
   _____

2. Read Galatians 3:28 and describe what God's view on prejudiceness is.
   _____
   _____
   _____

3. Read Genesis 2:24. Fill in the blanks. "Therefore a man should leave his father and mother and be joined to his wife, and _____ _____
   _____ _____ _____

4. In Genesis 2:18 what is your interpretation of *helper* in this verse? _____
   _____

MY JOURNAL

MY JOURNAL

Chapter 2

Biblical Women of The Bible

The first thing I would like to address is the biblical women in the Bible, and who they were in Christ. What were their roles in Christ? Before we can discuss about the roles of modern women we must first understand the roles of women in history.

This will be a short study to show what God has said about women, and how He has used women in His eternal plan. God placed great value on women. Let's look at **Genesis 1-27** again.

*"And God created man in His own image, in the image of God He created Him; male and female He created them. As you can see God created all humans. He created them equally! He told Adam **and** Eve to have dominion over the earth. In **Genesis 1:31** it says, "God saw all that He made, and behold it was good."*

He continues in **Genesis 18-25** to discuss the importance of Adam and Eve being together in one body as one. Marriage is very important in God's eyes. He didn't want Adam to be alone. He made Eve as a companion for Adam.

God also states in the fall of man how man and woman are given the responsibility to choose freely to obey or disobey God. In Genesis Sarah, Rebekah and Rachel had a place of dignity in which they could converse with men. Each woman found favor in God's eyes and had a special role for God's purpose.

In *Exodus 15:20, 21*, Miriam the Prophetess, Moses' sister, had a prophetic gift, a gift that came from God. This verse says, *"Then Miriam the prophetess, the sister of Aaron, took the timbrel in her hand; and all the women went out after her with timbrels and with dances, and Miriam answered them: Sing to the Lord, For he has triumphed gloriously. The horse and its rider He has thrown into the sea!"* She was giving God praise with music.

Judges 4:4 tells of Deborah who was a prophetess who was judging Israel at the time. She was the wife of Lapidoth.

Judges 4:5 says, "And she would sit under the palm tree of Deborah between Ramah and Bethel in the mountains of Ephraim. The children of Israel came to her for judgment. She deployed ten thousand men to go to Mt. Tabor. Barak wanted her to go with them so she did.

Esther 2:17 says that Esther was a beautiful orphan Jewish girl with a secret past who becomes the wife of a powerful King which made her the queen of Persia. Her husband wanted to kill the entire Jewish race because of Haman. Esther went to her husband, the king and pleaded for him to let her people live. This was a very courageous thing to do since; she could have been killed by going in front of her husband, the king, without being summoned. She had so much love for her people that she risked her own life to save them.

In the New Testament, Mary the mother of Jesus had awesome faith to what the angel was telling her in *Luke 1:38.*

What a great example of the honor shown to women than to have a woman be used by God to bring His Son into the world! He didn't have to do this; He chose to do this. He gave Mary the blessed gift to give birth to and raise His only Son!

Anna the prophetess spoke of the Messiah who would come to the temple in *Luke 2:36-38.*

Jesus interacted with many women. In *John 4:7-42*, He revealed His identity to an unnamed woman, many times married, who became the first Samaritan evangelist. Mary and Martha were also women of God.

These are just a few of biblical women the Bible speaks about. Among these women were also the virtuous women like Ruth *(Ruth 1:16, 17), Hannah, (I Samuel 1:8:28),* and many unnamed women in *Exodus 35: 20-29.*

Proverbs 31:10-31 speaks about women and their exalted and responsible roles as wives. These verses speak about how a virtuous wife is worth far above rubies and the heart of her husband safely trusts her**, vs. 10-11.**

The virtuous woman does her husband good and no evil all the days of her life, **v. 12.**

She works with her hands and brings her food from afar**, v. 14.**

She rises while it is yet night and provides food for her household, **vs. 15.**

She girds herself with strength**, vs. 17.**

She extends her hand to the poor and reaches out her hands to the needy, **vs. 20.**

She opens her mouth with wisdom and her tongue is the law of kindness, **vs. 26.**

She watches over the ways of her household and does not eat the bread of idleness, **vs. 27**.

Her children rise up and call her blessed, her husband also and he praises her, **vs. 28**.

But the woman who fears the Lord, she shall be praised, **vs. 30**.

Give her the fruit of her hands, and let her own works praise her in the gates.

The descriptions of the virtuous woman are only meant to be guidelines, not demands. Even though these verses talk about the household duties; the women also work outside the home. No ordinary woman can fulfill all the requirements as listed in Proverbs. We are just to be the best we can be.

God did not let our gender status be the basis for which He would talk with or for choosing the ministries He had planned for the women of the Bible. Jesus ministered with a woman who had bled for 12 years in *Mark 5:25-34*. She came to Him in the crowd just to touch the hem of His garment with total faith that she would be healed. In *Mark 5:35*, Jesus heard of the little girl who was dying and He took her hand and healed her immediately.

Read the following Scriptures for more examples of Jesus' love for women:

Matthew 15:21-25, then Jesus went out from there and departed to the region of Tyre and Sidon. And behold, a woman of Canaan came from that region and cried out to Him, saying, "Have mercy on me, O' Lord, Son of David! My daughter is severely demon-possessed." but He answered her not a word. And His disciples came and urged Him, saying, "Send her away, for she cries out after us." But He answered and said, "I was not sent except to the lost sheep of the house of Israel." Then she came and worshipped Him, saying, "Lord, help me!" **Verse 28** *says, "Then Jesus answered and said to her, "O woman, great is your faith! Let it be to you as you desire." And her daughter was healed from that very hour.*

John 4:5-30 *These verses talk about how Jesus asked a woman who was standing by the well for a drink of water. This woman was a social outcast and tried to avoid people as much as possible. Normally men did not speak to women in the public. Jewish men did not speak to Samaritan men, let alone Samaritan women. Jesus brought this woman's sin to light. She had been married 5 times and was living with a man who was not her husband. Jesus taught her about Himself and how He could change her life. He forgave her and saved her.*

John 8:1-11. *The religious leaders caught a woman in adultery and brought her before Jesus. She would have been put to death for an offense such as this, But Jesus did not condemn her but He did not condone what she had done either nor did He let it go. Jesus asked the religious leaders if they were without sin and they could not answer and left one by one. Jesus told the woman to go and sin no more. He forgave her. He saved her.*

Women were some of Jesus' closest friends. Some of these were Mary and Martha in ***Luke 10:38-42; John 11:1-46; 12:1-11***, and Mary Magdalene in ***Luke 8:1-3, John 19:25; 20:1,2 11-18; Matthew 27:55, 56; 28:1.*** Women's roles were very important in the biblical times. Women were among the 120 devoted to prayer in the upper room.

Women were evangelists just as men were. Jesus filled them with the Holy Spirit with the utterance to speak in tongues.

Jesus had many women in His life. Many women accompanied Him in His travels. Women were the first ones at His crucifixion and the first ones to discover His resurrection. They never left Jesus.

Matthew 28: 1-6 says, "In the end of the Sabbath, as it began to dawn toward the first day of the week, came Mary Magdalene and *the other Mary to see the sepulcher. And behold, there was a great earthquake, for the angel of the Lord descended from heaven, and came and rolled back the stone from the door, and sat upon it. His countenance was like lightning, and His raiment white as snow. And for fear of Him the keepers did shake, and became as dead men. And the angel answered and said unto the women, Fear not ye: for I know that ye seek Jesus, which was crucified, He is not here; for He is risen, as He said. Come, see the place where the Lord lay."*

The first one to talk to Jesus after He arose was a woman, Mary of Magdala:

"Jesus saith unto her, Mary. She turned herself, and saith unto Him, Rabboni; which is to say, Master. Jesus saith unto her, Touch me not; for I am not yet ascended to My Father; but go to My brethren and say unto them, I ascend unto My Father, and your Father; and to My God and your God. Mary Magdalene came and told the disciples that she had seen the Lord and that He had spoken these things unto her." **John 20:16-18 KJV.**

He never talked down to women or said anything to make them feel unequal to men. When Jesus was being crucified many of the men ran away leaving Jesus, but the women stayed with him till the end.

Matthew 27:55-56 says, *"And many women were there beholding afar off, which followed Jesus from Galilee, and ministering unto Him; Among which was Mary Magdalene, and Mary, the mother of James and Joses, and the mother of Zebedee's children.* **John 19:25** *states, "Now there stood by the cross of Jesus His mother, and His mother's sister, Mary the wife of Cleophas, and Mary Magdalene.*

These are just some of the examples of how much Jesus loves and depends on women. He wants not only men, but also women to follow the plans He has for us. God is not prejudice, far from it.

Scriptures are not just a list of rules but a witness of who Christ is. To understand who we are in Christ, we must first understand who Christ is Himself. We have to understand what Christ is about. Why Christ had come to this earth? What reason did God have to send us Jesus Christ? He wanted to save us by grace. He knew we couldn't be perfect. He had to make a way for us to make the right choice to love Him or not; both men and women. Jesus loves everyone! He loves those who did not love Him. He loves the little children. He loves men and women. He loves us all equally!

Jesus does not favor one gender over another. There are only believers, male or female.

Although God is not prejudice of women over men there is still the subject of position and status. We all have certain roles in our lives. We have roles of husband, son, father, mother, daughter, and wife.

Position and status must not be confused with role or function. For example, a husband and wife are equal before God but have different roles. Even though we are equal in Christ we have different functions.

Galatians 3:8 has a bearing on our position in Christ. *"There is neither Jew nor Greek, there is neither slave nor free, there is neither male nor female, for you all one in Christ Jesus."*

As we have studied about the biblical women as you can see, women do have a place in the Body of Christ. God is not prejudice.

He expects as much from women in their ministry as He does from men in theirs. When you are called of God He calls you for His plan.

Romans 8:28 *says, "And we know that all things work together for good to those who love God, and to those who are the called according to His purpose;* NKJV.

We all have a calling. Whether we are male or female we have to follow that calling. God used many women in biblical times and He has and will continue to use many women in modern times. He has called women to be ministers, evangelists, Sunday school teachers, pastoral counselors. Christian women every-where who have not been called into one of the above-mentioned ministries have still been called. All Christians are called to teach the Word of God, to their children, to their co-workers, to their friends, to anyone we come in contact with. Again, ***all Christians, male or female.***

Go to the Bible study and answer the questions. In the next chapter we will be discussing Women of God in the 21st century.

Read all Bible Scriptures throughout this chapter and pray to God for full understanding. Again this is only my interpretation of the Scriptures. Please make sure you read for your own understanding.

Pray this prayer:

Dearest Heavenly Father,

I want you to use me as you used the women in biblical times. I want to be a vessel for Your Glory. Show me what your plan for my life is. Give me listening ears as you give me instruction. Help me to be like the biblical women in the Bible. Help me to be a virtuous woman. Open my eyes to understand who you are Dear Lord as I am beginning to learn who I am in You.

In Jesus' Name
Amen.

Memory Scripture: Genesis 1:27; So God created man in His own image; in the image of God He created him; male and female He created them.

Chapter 2

Biblical Women of the Bible

Study Exercise 2

1. After studying the chapters given on Biblical women on page 9, what were some other women that followed God or that God used in the Bible? _____
   _____

2. Who were the women that stayed with Jesus throughout the crucifixion and resurrection? _____
   _____

3. What woman help to save the Jewish race? _____
   _____
   _____

4. What do the verses on a virtuous woman mean to you? ____
   _____
   _____

5. What are some things women do today to show that they are virtuous women? _____
   _____

6. In Romans 8:28 where it says all are called according to His purpose, what do you feel that called you to do? _____
   _____

7. Who was Miriam? _____
   _____

8. Who was the first woman Jesus talked to after He arose? _____
   _____
   _____

My Journal

My Journal

Chapter Three

Women In The 21ˢᵗ Century Becoming More Like Christ

In Proverbs we talked about the virtuous woman; that she is noble, a good, devoted wife, a hard worker, manager of wealth, and caring mother reaching out to the poor, and being praised by her family. We all know this is a very hard thing to accomplish and it would be unrealistic to think that any woman who wants to be virtuous can accomplish this. However, we have to look at this example of a virtuous woman to go by. This virtuous woman has reached perfection that seems impossible for the modern woman. Do we have to be perfect for God to accept us and love us? No, in fact Scripture teaches otherwise.

Romans 5:17 *says, "For if by one's man's offense death reigned through the one, much more those who receive abundance of grace and of the gift of righteousness will reign in life through the One, Jesus Christ.*

This verse shows us that God has given us grace to make up for the mistakes we make; although we have to be repentive and have a true desire to follow God's Word. We obviously cannot do what we want, and continuously defy God. We don't ever want to tempt God. We have to do the best we can to avoid temptation and do what God expects us to do as Christians.

God uses many people of all genders, races, and ages for His redemptive plan. Women are very valuable to God. He uses us to minister His Word, and to fellowship with. He uses us in our homes, churches and in the workplace. This is seen in Scripture. God treasures women.

*In **Judges 45:9** says, "Kings' daughters are among Your honorable women.* God called women honorable.

In **Luke 1: 27, 28**, God chose Mary to bear His Child, *"And having come in, the angel said to her, "Rejoice, highly favored one the Lord is with you; blessed are you among women.* God did not have to bring a Son into this world but He chose to. He chose it for man and woman.

In the 21st century, we know things have changed a great deal for women. There has been a lot of controversy on the roles of women since way back when the government would not allow women to so much as vote. Women were not allowed to work unless it was in the home. Women were expected to bear children, stay home and cook and clean and take care of the children. We were not allowed to have an equal role in the home or in church. Today, women have more freedom to work outside of the home, vote, run for president and government offices. Some women are the head of their households due to divorce. They are playing the roles of fathers and mothers for their children. Women have become ministers, evangelists, and Sunday school workers in their churches. Women now have a role in society and have always had a role in God's eyes. Women today, desire to have a career, a family, and enjoy other church

and community activities. Women of God should anchor their lives in truth of Scripture and try to live by the examples of the virtuous woman.

Some women of today live with very low self-esteem thinking they cannot live up to the standards their husband puts on them or the standards that they think God puts on them. Some women today find themselves depressed, unsatisfied in their lives and marriages. They feel alone and worth nothing. They live with daily struggles of working a job and raising the children and taking care of their husbands and often find themselves overexerted or strained. They seek a place of peace and a desire to find themselves. They may have everything their heart desires but still find themselves missing something. Being women of God we need to know how to live a successful life without feeling like there is something still missing.

Successful living guidelines:

Put God first.
It will by no means be easy with all the things we have to do in our daily lives with our careers, family and outside activities. We need to create an everlasting intimacy with God and make Him the priority in our life. As long as we put God above our husbands, children, and careers He will take care of the rest. He will take care of our husbands, children, and careers. I mentioned in the previous chapters that to know who we are in Christ, we have to **know** God rather than knowing **about** God. We have to give God our undivided attention and have an intimate relationship with God. We have to interact with God just as we interact with our families and friends. We have to find a place of solitude and be still to have a quietness in our spirits.

This will be the only way to hear God speak to our spirits through the Holy Spirit. We have to be willing to take time out to listen to Him

instead of Him listening to us. We often pray and we do all the talking but do we ever try to listen to Him talk? Do we care what God has to say? Yes, I think we do, except we don't know how to open our hearts and spirits to be able to hear Him. He's there; we just have to train ourselves to know how to listen for Him. This stillness will not only allow you to have a more personal relationship with God but it will give you inner peace in knowing He is there with you. You are not alone. So make Him your first priority.

Know the truth.

This requires us to put off our beliefs and educate ourselves to what the truth is according to the Bible. This requires knowing ourselves and getting in touch with our past. We have to put off the old body and become new.

2 Corinthians 5:17 states, "Therefore if anyone is in Christ Jesus, old things have passed away, behold all things become new."

We have to become new. We forgive the transgressors of others and we leave it in the past. For some who have gone through great abuse and neglect they should seek a Christian counselor to help them with this. We have to also be ready to allow God to show us our faults so they can be corrected. We don't always see things we do wrong and we have to be willing to allow this to come to truth. We will never be ready to commit ourselves to God without admitting our sins and repent. Then and only then can we start new.

Create Christian Relationships.

When we create Christian relationships within the church and outside of the church it keeps us strong. Humans need to have relationships for connection. Without this connectedness we would yield to depression. God knew that we would need people.

That is why He created women to begin with; so that Adam would not be lonely. We may choose to be alone at times and this is normal but where it begins to be a problem is when it causes you to feel totally isolated and disconnected. We begin to feel anxiety, sadness, and depression. However, we need to surround ourselves with Christian relationships. These types of relationships help us when we have depression, anxiety, and sadness because they help us regain our perspective according to Scripture. Other Christians can build us back up in our faith. When we are at the point of giving up we have other Christians to help us regain our strength.

John 15:13 says, *"Greater love hath no one than this, than to lay down one's life for his friends."*

Become more spiritually mature.

Peter's life was based around spiritual growth. Paul presented everyone to be perfect in Christ. Spiritual growth involves becoming an adult in Christ. Becoming mature in the Holy Spirit. It involves increasing our worship of Him, become humble, develop joy in our lives, becoming submissive to Christ, and developing courage.

2 Peter 1:5-10 lists some qualities of becoming spiritually mature. *"But also for this very reason, giving all diligence, add to your faith virtue, to virtue knowledge, to knowledge self-control, to self-control perseverance, to perseverance godliness, to godliness brotherly kindness, and to brotherly kindness love. For these things are yours and abound, you will be neither barren nor unfruitful in the knowledge of our Lord Jesus Christ. For he who lacks these things is shortsighted, even to blindness, and has forgotten that he was cleansed from his old sins.*

Therefore brethren, be even more diligent to make your call and election sure, for if you do these things you will never stumble; for so an entrance will be supplied to you abundantly into the everlasting kingdom of our Lord and Savior Jesus Christ."

We cannot come into spirituality under our own hand or power. We have to yield to the Holy Spirit. We have to turn our spirits over to God and allow Him to mold us. Growth is a gift from God. It isn't something we can control. In working to allow God to make us more spiritual we have to be disciplined, open yourself to Him. Studying and meditating on Scripture keeps our minds renewed.

Romans 12:2 *says, "I beseech you therefore, brethren, by the mercies of God, that you present your bodies a living sacrifice, holy, acceptable to God, which is your reasonable service. And do not be conformed to this world, but be transformed by the renewing of your mind, that you may prove what is that good and acceptable and perfect will of God."*

Again, we have to be silent and listen to God in prayer and worship. We have to be willing to worship, pray, service, give, and celebrate; these are the characteristics of believers who are wanting to grow spiritually. It creates joy, peace and love in our lives.

Spiritual friendships help us to grow spiritually. They help us gain perspective on what we are doing. They allow us to talk about our sins and help us to repent for them. They help us through our struggles by reminding us of the love that Jesus has for us; and the gift of spirituality He gives us. They keep us from temptations that plague us everyday. They rebuild hope in us when we fail. They offer us a safe place to come.

Spending time in church is another thing that helps us grow spiritually. We go to church to worship God and to fellowship with other Christians. We go to church to learn more about what God has planned for our lives and what Jesus has done for us. It reminds us of His unfailing love.

When we endure pain and trials we grow spiritually. Without

pain or suffering we would stay the same. We have to endure trials to learn from our mistakes. If we never had tribulation we would never know how to handle it. Trials, pain, and suffering help us to grow emotionally and spiritually. It helps us to become adults spiritually. God doesn't like us to have pain and suffering but it is a necessary part of life. It is something we will never be able to avoid because of the imperfect world we live in. We have to focus on keeping our faith in God that these things are necessary.

2 Timothy 4:7 says, "I have fought the good fight, I have finished the race, I have kept the faith. Finally there is laid up for me a crown of righteousness, which the Lord, the righteous judge will give me on that Day."

God does not make us perfect as soon as we accept Him. It is a process. He transforms us. We must always keep seeking to become more mature in Christ.

Dear Most Heavenly Father:

I thank You for Your many blessings. I thank You for creating me as a woman. I know I am very special in Your Eyes. I thank You for helping me to grow and mature spiritually. Continue, O Lord, to mold me. Help learn how to listen to You Father. Continue Your work in me. I want to be more like you. Thank You for helping me learn who I am in You.

In Jesus' Name,
Amen.

Memory Scripture: **2 Corinthians** *5:17: "Therefore if anyone is in Christ Jesus, old things have passed away, behold all things become new."*

Chapter 3
Women in the 21st Century
Becoming More Like Christ

Study Exercise 3

1. How have the views on women changed since the 1900's? ___
   _____
   _____

2. What are views on women in this day and age? _____
   _____
   _____

3. How have women suffered because of their view of themselves? _____
   _____
   _____

4. What are some ways we can work on our spiritual maturity? _
   _____
   _____

5. What does 2 Corinthians 5:17 say? _____
   _____

6. What does 2 Corinthians 5:17 say? _____
   _____
   _____

7. What are some ways we can work on our spiritual maturity?
   _____
   _____

8. What does Romans 12:2 say? _____
   _____
   _____

My Journal

My Journal

Chapter 4

Knowing God

Who is God? Do we ever take the time to really get to know God? We are usually so wrapped up in what we need from God that we don't think about what God needs from us? God put us here to have a relationship with Him; just as if we were having a relationship with our friends and family. He is our Father in Heaven. He is our Creator.

He desires us to fellowship with Him. He wants a relationship with us on His terms not ours. God loves those that have a relationship with Him and who truly love Him, but He also loves those that hate Him. He wants us to seek Him. He wants us to find Him. He makes it our free choice whether to accept Him or not.

Before women can know who they are in Christ they have to know Christ and who He is. We have to desire to know God better than we know ourselves. We have to thirst for a relationship with God. He has to be the priority in our lives. As long as we search for God only to solve our problems we will never truly know God. We have to have faith to know God. Since we can't see him we have to have faith that He is there.

Hebrews 11:6 says, "But without faith it is impossible to please Him, for he who comes to God must believe that He is, and that He is a rewarder of those who diligently seek Him.

Hebrews 11:1 says, "Now faith is the substance of things hoped for, the evidence of things not seen."

Hebrews 11:6 says, " By faith we understand that the worlds were framed by the word of God, so that the thing which are seen were not made of things which are visible."

Other Scriptures on faith are; *John 20:2, Matthew 6:30-34, Luke 17:5, Romans 3:22-28, Romans 5:1, Hebrews 12:2, and 2 Peter 1:1-9.* Take time to read these chapters.

Faith also gets our prayers answered. *Mark 5:34* talks about the woman who bled for 12 years and had the faith to know that if she could just touch Jesus' garment she would be healed.

We also have to have obedience to have our prayers answered. We have to be ready to prepare ourselves to do as God's Word says. We have to be obedient to the Heavenly Father just as we would be obedient to our earthly father. God cannot and will not answer our prayers when we are not obedient to Him.

We have to have faith in God to know who God is.

Exodus 20:1-3 says, " I am the Lord your God, who brought you out of the land of Egypt, and out of the house of bondage. You shall have no other gods before Me.

God wants

Psalms 14:2 says, "The Lord looks down from Heaven upon the children of men, to see if there are any who understand, who seek God."

God wants **us** to seek **Him**. He wants us to have a free choice to decide whether we serve Him or not. We are never forced into loving and serving Him.

The characters of those who may dwell with the Lord are stated in ***Psalms 15;*** *Lord, who may abide in Your tabernacle? Who may dwell in Your holy hill? He who walks uprightly, and works righteousness, and speaks the truth in his heart; He who does not backbite with his tongue, Nor does evil to his neighbor, nor does he take up a reproach against his friend; In whose eyes a vile person is despised, But he honors those who fear the Lord; He who swears to his own hurt and does not change; He who does not put out his money at usury, Nor does he take a bribe against the innocent.*

So who is God? God is the Eternal Word.

John 1 1-5 *describes who God is. "In the beginning was the Word, (God) and the Word was with God, and the Word was God. He was in the beginning with God. All things were made through Him, and without Him nothing was made that was made. In Him was life, and the life was the light of men. And the light shines in the darkness, and the darkness did not comprehend it.*

John 1:10 *says He was in the world, and the world was made through Him, and the world did not know Him. He came to His own, and His own did not receive Him. But as many as received Him, to them He gave the right to become children of God, to those who believe in His name; who were born, not of blood, nor of the will of the flesh, nor of the will of man, but of God.*

John 1: 14 *says, And the Word (God) became flesh (Jesus) and dwelt among us, and we beheld His glory, the glory as of the only begotten of the Father, full of grace and truth.*

We have grace and truth through the knowledge of Jesus Christ.

John 1:16-18 *says "And of His fullness we have all received, and grace for grace. For the law was given through Moses, but grace and truth came through Jesus Christ. No one has seen*

God at any time. The only begotten Son, who is in the bosom of the Father, He has declared Him.

God is the Word. When we read the Bible we are learning whom God is. We are learning through faith and grace. In ***John 14:6*** it gives another description of who God is.

*"Jesus said to Him, "I am the way, truth, and the life. No one comes to the Father except through me." **John 14:7** "If you had known Me, you would have known My Father also; and from now on you know Him and have seen Him.*

Jesus tells us here that when we know Him we know His Father. We can only come to the Father and truly know Him through Jesus Christ. This is who God is. He is the Word, the way, the truth, and the life.

Now that we know who God is we can know who we are in Him. God made His children many promises to express to us what we are to Him. These were unconditional promises with no conditions attached. He promised Abraham that His descendants would become a great nation and all the families would be blessed through him.

Genesis 12:1-3 *and* ***15:1-8*** *"And the Lord said to Abram, " Get out of your country from your family and from your father's house, to a land that I will show you. I will make you a great nation; I will bless you and make your name great; And you shall be a blessing. I will bless those who bless you, and I will curse those who curses you; And in you all the families of the earth shall be blessed."*

God promised Abraham He would bless his family and He kept His promise.

Another unconditional promise God has made to us is that,

"Whoever calls on the name of the Lord shall be saved, in ***Joel 2:32*** and again in **Romans *10:13***. The only way God could keep this promise is to give His only Son's life for those who believe.

In ***Hebrew 8:7-12*** God promises His presence with His people. Jesus says in ***Matthew 28:20****; I am with you always even to the end of the age.*

Jeremiah 1:5 tells us that God knew us in the womb and before we were born He sanctified us.

2 Peter 1:4 *says, " By which we have been given to us exceedingly great and precious promises, that through these you may be partakers of the divine nature, having escaped the corruption that is in the world through lust.*

Who are we in Christ? We are His children. He thinks of us the same way we think of our own children. We are created in His image. He loves us so much that He gave His only Son for us. You are someone special in God's life. He ordained you before you were ever born. God has shown us through His Word who He is. He has made a way for us. He is an all-powerful God and a loving Father. What better way to show us our value than to create us?

Dear Heavenly Father:

Thank you Lord for creating me. You have known me longer than I have known me. You planned my life for me. You gave your Son for me. You are the way, the truth and the life. Thank you for your grace and your salvation. I will praise you with my whole heart. Your work is honorable and glorious and your righteousness endures forever. You are gracious and full of compassion.

In Your Precious Holy Name,
Amen.

Memory Scripture: **Hebrews 11:1** *Now faith is the substance of things hoped for; the evidence of things not seen.*

Chapter 4

Knowing God

Study Exercise 4

1. What is the first thing we have to know before we can know who God is? _____

2. What do we have to have before we can know God? _____
   _____

3. What does Hebrews 11:1 say? _____
   _____
   _____

4. Who is God? _____
   _____

5. What promise did God make to Abraham? _____
   _____
   _____
   _____

6. Does this promise pertain to us today? _____

How? _____

_____

7. Who are we in Christ? _____

8. What does Jeremiah 1:5 say? _____

_____

_____

9. What does this verse mean to you? _____

_____

My Journal

My Journal

Chapter 5

Women: Who We Are in Marriage

So far, we have learned who God is, who we are as women in Christ, and how we can learn to know God. I would like to address the issue on marriage. What does God expect of women in marriage? What are our roles? Yes, God created man and woman equally but as I stated in earlier chapters we have different functions.

In earlier times, women's roles have been predominantly in the home, taking care of the children and household tasks, and the man was to go out and earn the income for the family. That is not the case now. More and more women are in the workplace for different reasons.

Some women have felt the need to work for financial reasons. Some have felt the need to work seeking a career for themselves.

What does God expect of women in marriage? Marriage is a covenant between two people and God. It is not necessarily about certain physical roles but emotional roles we have in marriage. He expects the husband and wife to love, cherish, protect and care for each other until death. So many marriage commitments today are made in vain. We don't take commitments seriously. But God does.

Commitment is a long-term covenant that should not be broken. We becomes one. "I" becomes "we."

Matthew 19:6 says, "They are no longer two but one flesh."

God knew this contract would be easily broken and never expected that a piece of paper would be enough to hold a marriage together. Long-term marriage demands more than a piece of paper to hold it together; it demands commitment; a bonding between two people ready to go the distance for better or worse. Many enter marriages thinking what is in it for me?

What can my spouse do for me; not what can I do for my spouse. We have to be ready to put our needs aside and focus on our partner's needs.

In the Old Testament times covenants were so serious that God held accountable those who broke the covenant. In Malachi, God identified marriage as a covenant that can't be broken without a very serious consequence.

Malachi 2:13-16 says, "You cover the altar of the Lord with tears, with weeping and crying; so He does not regard the offering anymore, nor receive it with goodwill from your hands. Yet you say, "For what reason?" Because the Lord has been a witness between you and the wife of your youth, with whom you have dealt treacherously; yet she is your companion and your wife by covenant. But did He not make them one, having a remnant of the Spirit? And why one? He seeks godly offspring. Therefore, take heed to your spirit, and let none deal treacherously with the wife of his youth.

A marriage covenant is a most sacred act for a man and woman. There is no such thing as a covenant without sacrifice. We have to sacrifice our needs everyday in marriage. This does not say that we deny our identity in marriage. Husband and wife both have their own identity just as they each have their own functions. The husband is not to strip the identity of the wife and the wife should never try to strip the identity from the husband.

We each have our own roles. To step in each other's roles would be wrong except in the case of single parenthood where the wife has to become the head of the household and vise versa. Many women have to take on this role in these times.

What is the main root cause of marital breakdown? Selfishness is the root cause of marital breakdown. We have to give up our wills while keeping our spirits in tact. We have to be willing to give our all to our spouses. It is no longer what can he or she do for me but how can I edify my spouse. When we do this then our spouse will reciprocate. You become one flesh in Christ and in marriage.

Matthew 19:4-6 states, "Have you not read that He who made them at the beginning made them male and female and said for this reason a man shall leave his father and mother and be joined to his wife, and the two shall become one flesh? So then, they are no longer two but one flesh. Therefore what God has joined together, let not man separate."

Ephesians 5:22-33 talks on the subject of marriage. We will go through each verse and discuss it.

Vs. 22 says, Wives, submit to your own husbands, as to the Lord.

Here the Bible says to submit to your husbands. What does He mean by submission? There has been a lot of controversy on the subject of submission. God is telling the wife to submit to her husband. This submission is a willing submission not a forced submission from her husband. In homes where there is a lot of domestic violence a woman is being forced to submit. Being forced to submit can lead to domestic violence and even death for a spouse who does not conform. Wives should submit to their husbands out of love and respect for him, because she loves God enough to do His will. Again it is a voluntary submission out of love and obedience to God but is never forced. The Bible teaches mutual submission in marriage. Husbands do for their wives and take care of them as they would take care of and love their own body. Wives should submit to their husband's leadership because that provides stability in the home. The only way we have permission from God to not submit to their husbands is if he is not Christian and willing to make decisions that are out of the line of God's Word. If the husband makes decisions that we as Christian women know are wrong in God's eyes and go against the teaching of God then we must then step in. This is the only way God releases us from submitting to our husbands. We as Christians are always to stay in line with the Word of God and never knowingly do what we know is against God.

Vs. 23-24 says, "For the husband is head of the wife, as also Christ is the head of the church; and He is the Savior of the body. Therefore just as the Church is subject to Christ, so let the wives be to their own husbands in everything.

Here the Bible is telling the husband that he is to be head over the wife. This means that he is by God held responsible for the family. It is his job to make sure that the household is run according to God's Word and in line with Scripture. He wants the husband to take responsibility of making sure he makes decisions on family matters that are in accordance with His Word.

Vs 25-27 says, Husbands, love your wives, just as Christ also loved the church and gave himself for her, that he might sanctify and cleanse her with the washing of water by the word, that he might present her to Himself a glorious church, not having spot or wrinkle or any such thing, but that she should be holy and without blemish.

Husbands should love their wives as Christ loved the church, meaning they would give up anything for the good of their wives.

When husbands love their wives this way then the wives will not be fearful in submitting to their husbands. Both spouses act in each other's best interest and live to please Christ. God expects husbands to guide the wife in a loving way. He is to encourage her, exalt her, and edify her, just as we are to do for our husbands.

__Vs. 28__ says, "So husbands ought to love their own wives Christ. God expects husbands to guide the wife in a loving way. He is to encourage her, exalt her, and edify her, just as we are to do for our husbands as their own bodies; he who loves his wife loves himself. For no one ever hated his own flesh, but nourishes and cherishes it, just as the Lord does the church.

God is telling husbands to love their wives as their own bodies. Husbands would never be abusive to their own bodies. Husbands take care of their bodies and love themselves. They are to love their wives as much as they love themselves. They are to nourish and cherish their wives. They are to take care of their wives as much as they take care of themselves.

__Vs. 33__ says: "Nevertheless let each one of you in particular so love his own wife as himself, and let the wife see that she respects her husband.

Even though God gives us guidelines pertaining to the marriage, He doesn't want us to be so wrapped up in the pleasing of our husband that it causes us to ignore our relationship with Him. We have to be diligent in making sure we do as God has commanded of us in our relationships but also be just as diligent in our relationship with Him.

Our roles as women in the marriage are based on God's covenant. We have to be committed to our relationships, not only with our families, but also with God. Our roles as women are to put Christ first in our lives. As long as we keep our relationship with God strong then we will have the desire to follow His instructions for our roles in marriage.

God doesn't mind if we work out of the home, or whether we work in the home as long as we can do both proficiently. He wants us to make sure we don't neglect our children and our marriage covenant, and most of all; our commitment to Him.

Consider the virtuous woman we talked about in the last chapter. This virtuous woman does her husband good, she works with her hands, and brings food from afar, she provides for her household, she watches over her household and raises her children. This virtuous woman is what women should strive for.

Another subject about the marital relationship is compromise. Marriage is full of compromises. We must learn to compromise with our spouses to avoid conflict. Compromise is another form of submission for both the husband and the wife. It is the idea of discussing decisions that need to be made and compromising with each other to come to the best conclusion. Compromise and submission go hand in hand. There will be decisions where a compromise cannot be made. As long as it is according to Scripture then the husband should be the one to make the final decision for the sake of the family. God holds the husband accountable for his role and the decisions he makes concerning the family.

We have discussed thus far who women are in Christ and the roles of women in the marriage covenant. In our next chapter we will be discussing the roles of women in a domestically violent marriage. Does Christ hold us to our marriage covenant when abuse is involved? We will find out.

Dear Heavenly Father,

I so desire to do your will. Teach me the ways of the virtuous woman. Give me the understanding I need on marriage covenant. Help me to be submissive to my husband out of my love for him and my love for You O' Lord. Help us to be submissive with each other. Help us to keep our covenant with each other as well as with You, Dear Lord. Do your will in our marriage to help us to become better partners and good examples for our children. Give my husband the wisdom to make good and right decisions for our family. Give him the strength he needs to be a good husband and a good father. Thank you for this very special covenant Father.

In Jesus' Name
Amen.

Memory Scripture: **Ephesians 5:33**. *Nevertheless, let each one of you in particular so love his own wife as himself, and let the wife see that she respects her husband.*

Chapter 5

Women: Who We Are In Marriage

Study Exercise 5

1. How have women's roles changed since the 1900's? _____
   _____
   _____

2. What does the term commitment mean to you? _____
   _____
   _____

3. How does God feel about covenants? _____
   _____

4. Read Malachi 2:13-16 and tell how God held accountable those who had broken the covenant. _____
   _____
   _____

5. What is the major root cause of marital breakdown besides finances? _____
   _____

6. What does Ephesians 5:22 say about submission? _____
   _____
   _____

7. Why should women submit to their husbands? _____
   _____

8. What type of submission is this? _____

9. What does Ephesians 5: 23-24 say about husbands? _____
   _____
   _____

10. What is another form of submission? _____

11. What are the roles of the husband in marriage? _____
    _____
    _____

My Journal

My Journal

Chapter 6

Women in Abusive Marriages

We discussed the woman's role in a normal-functioning marriage. But what happens if you're not in a normal-functioning marriage? What happens if you are in a very dysfunctional and abusive marriage? Does God hold us to the covenant and the commitment we made to our marriage partner?

Domestic violence is rampant in these last days. Marriages are being destroyed; wives and their children are being abused. Even though this is a very disturbing topic to discuss I feel we must touch on this subject.

Being a licensed pastoral clinical counselor this is a subject that must be discussed and dealt with. I urge women that if they are in a marriage where there is a great deal of violence to please seek immediate help whether it be from your pastor or a counselor, but please I urge you to seek the help of a professional that you can talk to and receive advice.

In these violent marriages there are several things going on. The husband may be a very controlling man, controlling every move of the woman with, who she can be friends with, whether she can see her family members or not, whether she can work outside of the home, or whether she can even use the phone. They usually stalk their wives when they are away from home and watching their every move and wanting to know what they doing every minute of every day. More often than not the wife is not   the only one who is being overly controlled, but the children are to. They are not permitted to do the simplest things such as, going outside to play, going to school, participating in school activities, having friends, and having friends over to their home for sleepovers. These marriages are full of violent beatings and abuse. Husbands emotionally, physically, and verbally abuse their family members.

That is not to say that there are not women who portray the same role in abusive marriages. There are some women who are very dominant in the marital relationship and take on the role of the husband and are very abusive. It goes both ways.

These women in these kinds of marriages are continually afraid to wake up in the mornings. They are afraid for their lives on a daily basis; usually afraid to take action such as leaving the marriage or getting law enforcement involved. Some women will tell you that they love their husbands and cannot bring themselves to filing charges against them or leaving; so they continue to live in these situations.

These women have very low self-esteem, thinking they are not good enough or that they can't make it on their own financially. They are so verbally abused they rarely can think on their own with the partner who is used to controlling and making every decision in the household. The husbands make sure they keep them in this state so they don't leave them.

Usually the children are deeply afraid of their father and have been told to keep things secret, so they are afraid to tell someone.

Does God require us to stay in these marriages with so much physical and emotional abuse? The answer to this question is an emphatic NO! God loves us and He requires our husbands to do the same. The husbands, who are often not saved, use the Scripture in the Bible on submission, thinking they have the right to treat their families this way. Most often than not, they only use this Scripture as a means of control especially if the woman is a believer, knowing that she wants to do the will of God.

Remember we talked about submission being a voluntary submission out of respect for their husbands and their love for God. This is by no means a forced submission. Spouses use this forced submission in the way of violence. So many women are being killed in these marriages when they disobey their husbands or do something he disagrees with. The beatings will get so bad that the husband ends up killing his wife and possible the children.

Husbands with this problem have such an anger built up inside them they are unable to understand how to release it other than beatings. They themselves have a very low self-esteem. They most often than not, have a lack of communication skills. They may have been abused as children and just doing what they were themselves taught.

Wives continue to stay in these relationships thinking things will get better or stop. Ladies, they don't and they can't get better unless God intervenes with healing for the man or he seeks counseling and truly desires to stop.

Can a marriage work out in these types of marriages? Can a wife expect things to stop? Sometimes. The husband must be willing to seek counseling. These relationships rarely heal on their own. After each episode of anger the husband will truly be remorseful and cry and try to assure the wife that he can stop. He won't and rarely ever does. The beatings only escalate becoming more and more violent. They never stop completely.

What does the Bible say on the subject of abuse? Let's look at the first Scripture on this subject. In the book of 2 Samuel 13:20 Tamar was raped by her half brother Amnon, and from that point on remained desolate in her brother Absalom's house.

In *Genesis 15:20,* Joseph is saying to his brothers who had thrown him in a pit to die, *But as for you, you meant evil against me; but God meant it for good.* God delivered Joseph out of that pit and went on to make him a very powerful man.

Ephesians 5:6-7 says, *Let no one deceive you with empty words, for because of these things the wrath of God comes upon the sons of disobedience, Therefore do not be partakers with them.*

Concerning the subject of marriage, let's take a look at Ephesians 5 again. *Ephesians 5:25-27* tells us, *Husbands, love your wives, just as Christ also loved the church and gave Himself for her, that He might sanctify and cleanse her with the washing of water by the word. That He might present her to Himself a glorious church, not having spot or wrinkle or any such thing, but that she should be holy and without blemish.*

Ephesians 5:28 says, "*So husbands ought to love their own wives as their own bodies; he who loves his wife loves himself. For no one ever hated his own flesh, but nourishes and cherishes it, just as the Lord does the church.*"

He is telling us that husbands do not hate themselves or beat themselves and they should treat their wives as they do their own bodies. No husband is going to control himself in the way he controls his wife. He is not going to abuse his own body the way he abuses his own wife. He is to love her as his own body; treating her with respect, love, and non-violence.

The abusing spouse usually abuses others because of their inability to communicate their feelings and their inability to express their anger in healthy ways. The anger a person has itself is not a sin, but the way we express our anger can be. When we allow our anger to get so out of control that we hurt someone else is not acceptable to God. *Ephesians 4:26 says,* "*Be angry and do not sin.*"

Women that are abused still love their husbands and they believe their husbands love them. Abuse is not love. Love is not supposed to hurt. The control a man uses over his wife is his own lack of self-esteem and desire to be respected and loved. He just goes about showing it the wrong way.

I Corinthians 13:4-8 states, *"Love suffers long and is kind; love does not envy; love does not parade itself, is not puffed up; does not behave rudely, does not seek its own, is not provoked, thinks no evil; does not rejoice in iniquity, but rejoices in the truth; bears all things, believes all things, hopes, all things, endures all things. Love never fails.*

Love is not supposed to hurt. Love is not about control. Love is not about submission. It is about God. It is about the commitment you make to God when you take a covenant of marriage. God does not want you to be in physical and emotional pain in your marriage.

When your husband breaks his covenant with God to love his wife as his own body then he has broken his commitment with you. He has released you. God does not expect for you to stay in a marriage of violence that could risk your life and the life of your children.

Remember we talked about how the wife is to respect her husband in his decisions of the household? I talked about the wife having to take the role of the husband in some decisions if the husband makes decisions for the household that are not in line of the Word. When the husband makes the decision to abuse the wife and her children then it is time to take an opposite position to make sure you and your children are protected. He does not hold you responsible for having to leave the marriage because of abuse.

If it is possible to get help or counseling for your husband then I say to separate yourself from the situation, allow him to seek counseling and finish counseling before returning to the home. I am all for saving a marriage if it can be saved. After all, I am a marriage counselor and I do believe that an abuser can be helped with anger management, but the husband or spouse has to be ready to make the decision to change. He has to get the help he needs and restore his relationship with God for spiritual healing.

It is imperative to remove the children from the home of the abuser not only to protect them, but, to help them break the cycle of abuse. This is a learned behavior and is highly contagious. When children do not see healthy ways of handling anger then they just do what they have seen and what they know. So I urge you women who are in abusive relationships to get out. If the marriage can be saved then each of you need to seek counseling while being separated then return to the home after the healing comes. Don't wait till it is too late. God loves you. You are a child of the King. You are a woman He made to be loved by her husband. You are important. He has a calling for you. You may help others by your experiences.

I urge you to seek the help of a professional, support from family members, and guidance from God. He is there for you and will protect you.

Seek a women's shelter in your area for help. The National Domestic Violence Hotline number is 1-800-299-7233 TDD 1-800-787-3224 if you need advice or for more information of services in your area.

This prayer has been provided for you to pray along with for the courage to take that first step and call someone. I know it will be very difficult, but once you make that decision, your spouse may seek help for himself. Usually once the wife leaves the marriage or sends the abusive spouse from the house then the abuser will do what it takes to save his marriage. Just because you may become separated does not necessarily mean you will be divorced. It just lets the abuser hit rock bottom, which is necessary for them, to seek the help they need. You may want to think about getting a restraining order for the spouse to leave the house if you have children. This will only help you to be able to keep your children in their home instead of going to a shelter. Of course, this has to be a decision you make with much guidance from God. Good luck! You are in my prayers.

Dear Lord,

You know my situation in my marriage Lord. You know the abuse I suffer everyday along with the abuse my children suffer everyday. Lord, give me the guidance I need to save my marriage if it can be saved. Lead me in the direction you would have me to take. Give me the courage to take that first step I need to take. I know you would not want me to live this way. I want to remain in your will, O Lord, so please give me your guidance. Protect us each day. Help me to yield to your Spirit.

In Jesus' name,
Amen

Memory Scripture: **Ephesians 5:28;** *So husbands ought to love their own wives as their own bodies; he who loves his wife loves himself.*

Chapter 6
Women in Abusive Marriages

Study Exercise 6

1. What do marriages with domestic violence consists of? __
   _____
   _____

2. Why do women stay with an abusive spouse? _____
   _____
   _____

3. Why does an abuser abuse their spouse? _____
   _____
   _____

4. Does God require us to stay in abusive relationships? ____
   _____
   Why? _____
   _____

5. What does Ephesians 5:25 say? _____
   _____
   _____

6. What does the Bible say about anger? _____
   _____
   _____

7. What does 1 Corinthians 13: 4-8 say about love? _____
   _____
   _____
   _____

8. Where can an abused spouse go to get help? _____
   _____

My Journal

My Journal

Chapter 7

Women: Who We Are As Mothers

This chapter will be about understanding who women are as mothers. What does God require of us as mothers? What does the Word say about the role of mothers? The following topics are the functions of mothers, as parents.

The first thing we as mothers need to remember is to nurture our children. We must bond with them from birth so that they may feel our love for them. We must not only feed them physically but also emotionally, spiritually, mentally, and socially. We have to help them learn how to have fun and play, how to pray to God, how to socialize with others, how to handle their anger, how to handle life hardships, how to express themselves when they are sad, how to laugh, how to recover from grief and to listen to others, how to learn, how to communicate and teach them about who God is.

We have to let them know we are there to protect them at all times and that God is there to protect them also. They have to feel secure in their lives. We have to protect them without over-protecting them. We have to help them to depend on us without being too dependent on us. We have to help them learn to depend on God. We have to help them be independent without taking away all their boundaries. Children need these boundaries. We have to help them to be able to be on guard of danger.

In this society, this has become an overwhelming problem. We have to protect their minds against false religious beliefs, bringing them up in the way of the Lord.

Proverbs 22:6 *says, Train up a child in the way he should go and when he is old he will not depart from it.*

We have to make sure they are educated. It is good to make sure which school or day-care is better than the other, but we must make sure our children trust us. They have to know that we can be trusted in responding to their needs and that we will always be there for them. Children need to not only go to school and learn the basics of reading, writing and arithmetic, but also learn the boundaries that life has for us. Children will always test these boundaries but having these boundaries is one way our children know we love them. They have to be educated in the Word of God. We must also be an example to them not only as parents, since they will be developing their parenting skills from us, but also as Christians. We have to be that positive role model in their lives. We need for them to look to us as their heroes and not replace us with the people they may see on T.V. We must be their role models whom they will want to model after in their adult life.

We will need to make sure we teach them about who God is. After all, we have been learning in this Bible study that until we know who God is we will never know who we are. We have to teach them about who they are in Christ.

We will need to make sure we raise them to be independent adults so they will later be able to leave their mother and father and cling to their spouses. They will need to be given a certain amount of independence as they grow and teach them decision-making and problem solving skills so they will use these as they become adults. We will need to be teaching them responsibility by assigning them tasks to do around the house, instructing them how to do these tasks without teaching them to be perfectionists that may later harm them. We will need to show and teach them appreciation. We need to let them know how much they are appreciated and loved so they may be able to do the same with their children.

What does the Bible say about child discipline? We are to love our children and at the same time know they will not always like us for disciplining them. There are parents who will withhold discipline and over-indulge the child simply because they want their children to love them. Parents, it is not our job to be their best friend, we have to be their parents first and when we do this we are showing our children how much we love them and then they will consider us to be their best friend. They will not always like us for our discipline but it will come later. We have to be able to allow them to talk to us about any topic so that we know what problems they are having and provide them with help for that problem. When our children feel they can confide in us about anything then this can prevent them from having to keep secrets and later destroying their lives with whatever they are unable to handle alone.

The Bible tells us of the importance of parental instruction and correction. We will have to deal with misbehavior by using corrective discipline. Does this mean we will always need to spank the children? No, although the Bible does tell us in **Proverbs 22:15** that says,

Foolishness is bound up in the heart of a child; the rod of correction will drive it far from him.

However, this does not mean we are to beat our children. Good parents will know when to use this method. If you are a parent that becomes angry to quickly and loses their temper then this method may not be for you. It is okay to spank our children but not abuse our children and we will never want to use this method while we are angry. This method should only be used for willful disobedience and not for childish irresponsibility.

In ***Proverbs 23: 13, 14*** it says, *Do not withhold correction from a child.*

Discipline is an act of love. It shows our children that we love them. Again, we are never to discipline our children out of anger. There are different discipline methods and parents who may not feel that they agree with the idea of spanking their children can adopt these other methods. Whatever the method, parents please use something. Don't allow your child to grow up without any parental supervision or correction.

Ephesians 6:1-4 says, *"Children, obey your parents in the Lord for this is right. Honor your father and mother, "which is the first commandment with promise, that it may be well with you and you may live long on the earth. And fathers, do not provoke your children to wrath, but bring them up in the training and admonition of the Lord.*

God wants us to bring up our children in the Lord and to teach them respect for parent's authority and have respect for others, but we are to never bring them to wrath. This means in the way of demeaning them or tearing down their self-esteem. We are to break their will of disobedience while keeping their spirits intact.

God expects us to keep ourselves healthy emotionally, and spiritually so that we may be able to take care of our children's spiritual and emotional, and physical needs. No other time than now have our children been in so much turmoil. We have to be vigilant in keeping our children safe and feeling secure in our love for them. Children are being abused, emotionally, physically, sexually, and spiritually in these last days more than ever. Our children are being left alone in their homes while parents work without supervision and this makes them vulnerable to people who may want to take advantage of your child. Our children should not have to be subjected to all the abuse they are having to endure. We as parents have to take a stand for all children and be there not only for our children but children who may not have the same Christian family life. It is our job as Christian mothers to be there for these abused and neglected children. Pray for our children.

God has given and trusted us with one of His most precious assets; our children. They are not only our children; they are His children. He requires us to make sure we raise them as He would raise them. He has trusted you to be a Godly parent. He expects you to raise your child in the Word of God. God loaned us our children for us to raise. They belong to Him. We have to make sure as mothers that we provide our children with every chance in the world to become a valiant and healthy child of God; healthy in every way; emotionally, spiritually, and mentally. God has a ministry and a planned future ahead for your child and it is up to us to keep the Word of God and raise them accordingly.

Our children have to be raised with the ability to love others and have compassion for others or the cycle of abuse will never end. If we as parents make sure we take care of our emotional and spiritual needs so that God can work in us and heal us of our past baggage that we bring into our marriages then we will be better parents and role models for our children.

Prayer:

Dearest Heavenly Father,

I come you today to thank you for giving me my children. Thank you for trusting me to raise your children. I pray to you Dear God, that you work through me to raise a valiant and healthy child for your service. Give me the knowledge I need as a mother to do the best job I can for you and my child. Give me the guidance of the Holy Spirit to be a good parent and role model for my child. Thank you God for trusting me with this important task and entrusting your children to me.

In Jesus' Name
Amen

Memory Scripture: **Proverbs 22:6;** *Train up a child in the way he should go and when he is old he will not depart from it.*

Chapter 6

Women: We Are As Mothers

Study Exercise 6

1. What is the first thing we as mothers need to remember to do for our children? _____

2. Name five things we as mothers need to make sure we teach our children? _____ _____
   _____ _____ _____

3. What is the **most important** thing to teach your child? ____
   _____

4. What does Proverbs 22:6 say about our responsibility as parents? _____
   _____

5. What is an important thing children need to feel loved? ____
   _____

6. How would we teach our children about responsibility? ____
   _____

7. What does Proverbs 22:15 say? _____
   _____
   _____

8. Discipline is an act of _____

9. What does Ephesians 6:1 say? _____
   _____
   _____

10. What does Ephesians 6:4 say? _____
    _____
    _____

My Journal

My Journal

Chapter 8

Salvation

We have learned about our roles as women in Christ, the home, the marriage, and as mothers and how to really know who God is. We studied about the biblical women of the Bible and how important they were to Jesus. The only thing left to touch on then would be our salvation in Christ.

How do we know we are saved? Because the Bible says we are. To be saved means to avoid permanent damnation in hell. It means to be delivered from our sins and accept Jesus Christ as our Lord and Savior. It means we have to put off the old body and become new in Christ Jesus.

2 Corinthians 5:17 tells us, *Therefore, if anyone is in Christ, he is a new creation; all things pass away, therefore all things become new.*

We have to be prepared to take off the old body and put on the armor of God. We have to allow our past to pass away and become a new creation.
We have to live the rest of our lives for Him and only Him.

John 3:16 tells us how much God loves us and what sacrifice He made for us.

For God so loved the world that He gave His only begotten Son, that whosoever believeth in Him would not perish but have everlasting life.

This is a major statement! He gave His only Son Jesus for our lives, so that we would be able be saved. He died in our place, for us; something we did not even deserve. Accepting Jesus Christ is the only way to go to Heaven and be saved. There is no other way.

Acts 4:12 says, *"Nor is there salvation in any other, for there is no other name under heaven given among men by which we must be saved.*

There is no other way. We have to go through Jesus Christ. There is no one that does not need to be saved. We all need to accept Jesus. Even after we have been saved we still need ongoing forgiveness from God. We will never be perfect. We will never have reached the heights of perfection that Jesus has.

Romans: 3:23 says, *"For all have sinned and fallen short of the kingdom of God.*

We will never reach that perfection. We are saved by His loving grace. Our spiritual condition is described in ***Isaiah 64:6,*** *But we are all like an unclean thing, and all our righteousnesses are like filthy rags. We all fade as a leaf, and our iniquities, like the wind, have taken us away.*

In ***Luke 19:10*** we are described as lost.

For the Son of Man has come to seek and to save that which was lost."

In **John 3:18** it says, *"he who believes in Him is not condemned; but he who does not believe is condemned already, because he has not believed in the name of the only begotten Son of God."*

And in **John 12:40** it describes us as blind. *He has blinded their eyes and hardened their hearts, Lest they should see with their eyes, Lest they should understand with their hearts and turn, so that I should heal them.*

Unless we humble ourselves and receive Christ we will not be saved. It is not something we can do ourselves. It comes from His grace. Only God can forgive us our sins. There is no other way around it.

God loves us so much that He sent His Son to save us. We are worth that much to Him. He sent His Son to die for us while we were still sinners!

Romans 5:8 it says, *"But God demonstrates His own love toward us, in that while we were still sinners. Christ died for us."*

While we were still sinners; He loved us that much!

2 Corinthians 5:21 says, *"For He made Him who knew no sin to be sin for us, that we might become the righteousness of God in Him."*

Jesus knew no sin but still took the cross and all the abuse He suffered for us, even though we were still sinners. He took our place on the cross.

1 John 4:9-10 says, *"In this the love of God was manifested toward us, that God has sent His only begotten Son into the world that we might live through Him.*

Vs. 10; *In this love, not that we loved God, but that He loved us and sent His Son to be the propitiation for our sins.*

Notice, where it says in verse 9 that we might live through Him; we can only be saved through Him. You have to accept Him. ***In verse 10*** it says *that not that we loved God, but that He loved us.* Jesus was not accepted. Many people wanted Him to be crucified. They never loved Him but He still loved them so much that He took this great sacrifice of His life.

1 Peter 3:18 shows how much Jesus loved us. *"For Christ also suffered once for sins, the just for the unjust, that He might bring us to God, being put to death in the flesh but made alive by the Spirit.*

He suffered a terrible death. He suffered greatly before being hung on the cross. He loved us that much! He suffered for the ones who didn't deserve His love, the ones who crucified Him. He suffered for all sinners.

The death of Jesus secured our salvation. If God had not given His only Son, we would not have a chance to be saved. We would have to be measured on our own ability, and we all know that we would fail tremendously. Jesus loves you. You matter to Him. He gave the ultimate price for us. We should give the ultimate price for Him. We should come to know God and accept Jesus as our Savior.

The name Jesus means "Savior" and derived from the ancient Hebrew Jehoshua. The title Christ means anointed, consecrated, sacred, and is used only for the Messiah, who came in fulfillment of prophesy.

God knew before Jesus was born what His purpose would be upon this earth so that we would have salvation.

The Hebrew term for salvation in the Old Testament is yeshu'ua, describing deliverance from distress. The New

Testament uses the Greek word soteria, a term that includes not just deliverance, but God's forgiveness of sins.

Romans 1:16 states, *"For I am not ashamed of the gospel of Christ, for it is the power of God to salvation for everyone who believes, for the Jew first and also for the Greek."*

We can't be ashamed of the Gospel of Christ. We shouldn't want to be ashamed of it. We should shout it from the housetops. We should want to see everyone we meet saved. We should never be ashamed of the Savior who gave His life for us. We did not deserve the great gift that God sent us.
We can never receive salvation any other way than through Jesus Christ. He gave us salvation through grace.

The Hebrew word for grace is *chen*; and in Greek, *charis* and means favor; kindness towards mankind shown by the Lord Jesus Christ. We can't earn favor or grace. We don't even have to; because it is freely given by God., *to them He gave the right to become children of God, to those who believe in His name.*

To those that believe in His name, we have to have faith and believe in Jesus Christ. We have to believe that **Ephesians 2:8** states this; *For by grace you have been saved through faith, and that not of yourselves; it is the gift of God.*

It is a free gift from God. It cannot be earned through anything we do. We have to have faith in God to receive it. God gives us redemption through Jesus Christ.

John 1:12 says, *"But as many as received Him* He died for our sins. This takes great faith. Since we cannot see Him we have to have faith that He is there and did this wonderful thing for humanity. We just have to reach out to Him. We have to accept Him. We have to believe in Him. We have to ask forgiveness for our sins and accept Him as our Lord and Savior.

This is a free gift for anyone. All we have to do is ask for it. You matter to Him. He paid a great price for us. This is how much God loves us.

Please ask Him into your life. Let Him be a part of your celebration of who you are in Christ Jesus.

Hebrews 4:16; *"Let us come boldly to the throne of grace, that we may obtain mercy and find grace to help in time of need."*

Won't you come boldly to the throne of Christ? Accept Him as your Lord and Savior. Jesus says in *John 7:37*, saying *"If anyone thirsts, let him come to Me and drink. Verse 38 says, He who believes in me, as the Scripture has said, out of his heart will flow rivers of living water."*

Romans 10:9-10 says that if you confess with your mouth the Lord Jesus and believe in your heart that God has raised Him from the dead, you will be saved. For with the heart one believes unto righteousness, and with the mouth confession is made unto salvation."

Romans 10:13 says, Whoever calls on the name of the Lord shall be saved."

If you have never asked Jesus Christ to be your Savior, you can ask Him right now by praying this prayer.

Dear Heavenly Father:

I know that I am a sinner. I know I need forgiveness for my sins. I know how much Jesus loves me to give His life for me. I believe that Jesus died on the cross and was buried in the tomb and arose again for me Lord. I come to you Father in the Name of Jesus for forgiveness. Save me by your grace O Lord. I accept Jesus Christ as my Lord and Savior and my free gift of grace and salvation. Thank you mighty God for loving me so much! I promise to live my life for you.

In Jesus' Name
Amen.

Memory Scripture: **John 3:16;** *"For God so loved the world that He gave His only begotten Son that whosoever believeth in Him should not perish but have everlasting life."*

Chapter 8

Salvation

Study Exercise 8

1. How do we know we are saved? _____
   _____

2. What does 2 Corinthians tell us? _____
   _____

3. What does John 3:16 say? _____
   _____
   _____

4. What is the only way to get to Heaven? _____
   _____

5. Romans 3:23 says, For all have _____ _____
   _____ _____ of the kingdom of
   God."

6. Romans 5:8 says, "But God demonstrates His own love
   toward us in that while we were _____
   _____ Christ died for us.

7. What does the name Jesus mean? _____

8. The title Christ means _____, _____, _____ and is used only for the _____.

9. What is the Old Testament Hebrew term for salvation?
   _____

10. What is the New Testament Greek term for salvation? ___
    _____

11. What is the Hebrew word for grace? _____

12. What is the Greek word for grace? _____

13. What does grace mean? _____

14. Ephesians 2:8 says, "For by grace you have been saved through faith, and that not of yourselves? _____
    _____ _____ _____
    _____, _____

15. What does Romans 10:13 say? _____
    _____

16. Have you accepted Jesus Christ as your Lord and Savior?
    _____

My Journal

My Journal

NOTES

NOTES

NOTES

NOTES

www.ingramcontent.com/pod-product-compliance
Lightning Source LLC
Chambersburg PA
CBHW032059150426
43194CB00006B/577